Victorian Colored Glass

2

Patterns & Prices

by

william heacock

Lithography by
Richardson Printing Corporation
Marietta, Ohio

I.S.B.N. #0-915410-13-3

Published & Distributed by

Antique Publications, Inc.
P.O. Box 655
Marietta, Ohio 45750

TABLE OF CONTENTS

INTRODUCTION

This pocket book is a miniaturized reprint of many of the color illustrations shown in the fourth and fifth volumes of the "Encyclopedia of Victorian Colored Pattern Glass," as well as the colored glass examples shown in my book "1,000 Toothpick Holders." As a special bonus, I am also including two dozen additional color pages from future Heacock books which have been delayed for various reasons.

Pattern names and estimates of retail value are provided. However, none of the text, historical data, dates of production, ad and catalogue reprints, non-glass items, or illustrations of reproductions are provided. This information is available only in the full-size books. An ad for these larger volumes is included in the back of this book.

The purposes for producing this tiny book were two-fold. It makes it possible for readers of Heacock books to own a handy pocket size edition for carrying to antique shows, flea markets, shops and auctions, thus saving wear and tear on the larger volumes. Also, the larger volumes are expensive to produce, and thus harder on the readers' budget. This less expensive smaller book makes it possible to expand the number of "informed" glass collectors and dealers, as a wealth of illustrations and pattern names are now available to those who hesitated investing in the larger volumes. Those earlier books will continue to be revised, updated and reprinted for those who wish to delve deeper into the information available on the glass illustrated here.

Generally, there should be little confusion in using this book. An index is provided at the back which will refer you to every pattern and art glass color which you might see advertised with a Heacock reference number. The only area where care should be taken is using the figure numbers correspondingly with the appropriate volume number. The same numerical system is used in every Heacock book, so the book title or volume number should always precede the figure numbers to prevent confusion. Also, the last 24 color plates in this new book are **new** pictures not shown in previous publications, so take note that you should refer to **this** book, with the appropriate page number.

Another word of warning. The prices provided are an estimate of general retail value. Prices always vary from area to area, from dealer to dealer. Value is determined by how many people with how much money want an item how badly. The "Three C's" — color, condition and collectability — also determine the prices. The prices quoted are for pieces in mint condition, and apply only to those colors illustrated in each pattern. Another color may be more or less desirable, and thus worth more or less.

A rarity guide is also provided. If only a limited number of a certain item is known, it is labelled (S) Scarce. If only two or three are known, it earns a desirable (R) Rare. If only one has been documented to date, it is most decidedly a Very Rare (VR) piece of glass. How rare an item is usually adds a little value to many pieces illustrated here.

Encyclopedia of
Victorian Colored Pattern Glass
Book 4

Custard Glass

From A to Z

by william heacock

Custard Glass by

Northwood & Associates

Including Patterns Made by:
The Northwood Co., Indiana, Pa.
H. Northwood & Co., Wheeling, W. Va.
Dugan Glass Co., Indiana, Pa.
Diamond Glass-Ware Co., Indiana, Pa.

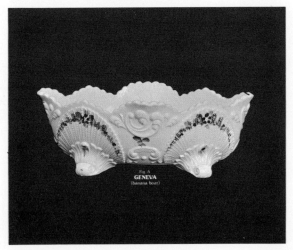

Fig. A
GENEVA
(banana boat)

A – $145.

Inverted Fan & Feather (W)

PUNCH BOWL & CUPS

1 — $2500 (VR); **2** — $275.

Inverted Fan & Feather (W)

3	4	3	5	6	5
SALT	JELLY	PEPPER	TUMBLER	PITCHER	TUMBLER

7	8	9	10
BUTTER	SUGAR	SPOONER	CREAMER

11	12	13	14	13
TOOTHPICK	CRUET (o.s.)	BERRY	MASTER BERRY	BERRY

3 — $400 pr. (R); 4 — $245 (S); 5 — $75; 6 — $375; 7 — $235; 8 — $165; 9 — $100; 10 — $100; 11 — $575; 12 — $600 (S); 13 — $55.

Northwood Grape

15
HATPIN HOLDER

16
TUMBLER

17
PITCHER

16
TUMBLER

18
COLOGNE

19
PIN TRAY

20
SPOONER

21
BUTTER

22
SUGAR

23
CREAMER

24
BREAKFAST SUGAR

25
BREAKFAST CREAMER

26
BERRY SAUCE
(pedestalled)

27
MASTER BERRY

28
BERRY SAUCE

14 — $185; **15** — $350 (R); **16** — $60; **17** — $325; **18** — $385; **19** — $110; **20** — $85; **21** — $195;
22 — $125; **23** — $85; **24** — $75; **25** — $75; **26** — $45; **27** — $165; **28** — $40.

CUSTARD GLASS BY NORTHWOOD & ASSOCIATES

Northwood Grape

30
PUNCH CUP

29
PUNCH BOWL

30
PUNCH CUP

31
FERNERY

32
HUMIDOR

33
CENTERPIECE BOWL

34
2-HANDLED NAPPY

35
8" PLATE
(six-sided)

36
8" PLATE

29 — $750 (R); **30** — $60; **31** — $275; **32** — $500 (R); **33** — $325 (S); **34** — $45; **35** — $48; **36** — $55.

Northwood's Grape

Grape Arbor

37
PUNCH CUP
(blue decor.)

38
PUNCH BOWL
(blue decor.)

39
TUMBLER
(pink stain)

40
PITCHER
(pink stain)

39
TUMBLER
(pink stain)

41
CRACKER JAR

42
ORANGE BOWL
(pink stain)

43
HUMIDOR
(pink stain)

44
ORANGE BOWL
(flat-top)

45
DRESSER TRAY

46
BANANA BOAT

37 — $75 (S); **38** — $1100 (VR); **39** — $80 (S); **40** — $525 (R); **41** — $425 (S); **42** — $325; **43** — $475 (R); **44** — $275; **45** — $295 (S); **46** — $275.

Intaglio (OMN)

47
CRUET
(o.s.)

48
TUMBLER

49
PITCHER

48
TUMBLER

50
BUTTER

51
SPOONER

52
BUTTER

53
SUGAR

54
CREAMER

55
SALT

55
PEPPER

56
MASTER BERRY

57
BERRY SAUCE

58
JELLY

47 – $250; **48** – $60; **49** – $275; **50** – $200; **51** – $95; **52** – $220; **53** – $140; **54** – $95; **55** – $145; **56** – $150; **57** – $45; **58** – $95.

Intaglio (OMN)

Everglades

59	60	61	62
LARGE FRUIT COMPOTE	TUMBLER	PITCHER	JELLY

63	64	65	66
SPOONER	BUTTER	SUGAR	CREAMER

67	68	69	70	69
SAUCE	MASTER BERRY	SALT (not custard)	CRUET (o.s.)	PEPPER

59 — $225; **60** — $75; **61** — $375 (S); **62** — $175 (S); **63** — $110; **64** — $225; **65** — $150; **66** — $110; **67** — $55; **68** — $225; **69** — $250 pr.

Chrysanthemum Sprig (K)

70 CELERY VASE	71 TUMBLER	72 PITCHER	73 CRUET SET	74 TOOTHPICK
75 SPOONER	76 BUTTER	77 SUGAR	78 CREAMER	
79 CRUET (blue opaque)	80 JELLY	81 MASTER BERRY	82 SAUCE	

70 – $550 (R); **70A** – $395 (R); **71** – $55; **72** – $375 (S); **73** – $800; **74** – $220; **75** – $100; **76** – $220; **77** – $150; **78** – $95; **79** – $600; **80** – $110; **81** – $185; **82** – $55.

CUSTARD GLASS BY NORTHWOOD & ASSOCIATES

Northwood Beaded Circle (PN)
(Figures 136-144)

136 SPOONER	137 BUTTER	138 SUGAR	139 CREAMER	140 PITCHER

141 SALT	142 CRUET (6 x.)	143 PEPPER	144 MASTER BERRY	145 SALT	146 CRUET	147 PEPPER	148 MASTER BERRY

Jackson
(Figures 145-152)

149 TUMBLER	150 PITCHER	149 TUMBLER	151 SUGAR	152 CREAMER

136 − $100; **137** − $275 (S); **138** − $160; **139** − $100; **140** − $385 (R); **141** − $180 ea. (S); **142** − $550 (R); **143** − $180; **144** − $210; **145** − $60; **146** − $160; **147** − $60; **148** − $135; **149** − $48; **150** − $230; **151** − $110; **152** − $95.

Geneva

153	154	155	154	156	157
JELLY	TUMBLER	PITCHER	TUMBLER	CRUET (o.s.)	SYRUP

158	159	160	161	162
SPOONER	TOOTHPICK	BUTTER	SUGAR	CREAMER

163	164	165	166	167
MASTER BERRY (oval)	SAUCE (oval)	SALT	SAUCE (round)	MASTER BERRY (round)

153 – $80; **154** – $55; **155** – $195; **156** – $250; **157** – $275; **158** – $75; **159** – $95; **160** – $160; **161** – $110; **162** – $80; **163** – $80; **164** – $35; **165** – $60; **166** – $45; **167** – $120.

Grape & Gothic Arches (Pr)

| 168 FAVOR VASE | 169 GOBLET | 170 TUMBLER | 171 PITCHER | 170 TUMBLER |

| 172 SPOONER | 173 BUTTER | 174 SUGAR | 175 CREAMER |

Double Loop (Pr)

| 176 BREAKFAST SUGAR (open) | 177 BREAKFAST CREAMER | 178 SAUCE | 179 MASTER BERRY |

168 — $75; **169** — $60; **170** — $48; **171** — $235; **172** — $70; **173** — $175; **174** — $100; **175** — $75; **176** — $75 (R); **177** — $75 (R); **178** — $80 (VR); **179** — $175.

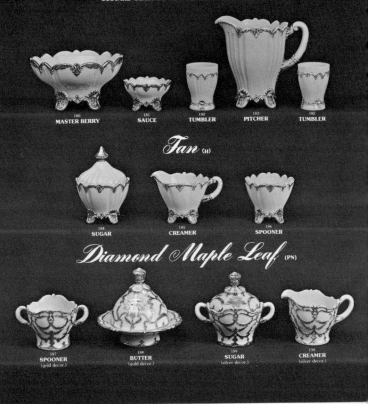

Fan (H)

Diamond Maple Leaf (PN)

180
MASTER BERRY

181
SAUCE

182
TUMBLER

183
PITCHER

182
TUMBLER

184
SUGAR

185
CREAMER

186
SPOONER

187
SPOONER
(gold decor.)

188
BUTTER
(gold decor.)

189
SUGAR
(silver decor.)

190
CREAMER
(silver decor.)

180 — $175; 181 — $50; 182 — $75; 183 — $250; 184 — $125; 185 — $85; 186 — $85;
187 — $95; 188 — $225 (R); 189 — $150 (S); 190 — $90.

Custard Novelties

191	192	193	194	195
THREE FRUITS	GOOD LUCK	DRAPERY	POINSETTIA LATTICE	SINGING BIRDS

196	197	198	199	200	201
DANDELION	BUSHEL BASKET	FINECUT & ROSES	BEADED CABLE	GRAPE ARBOR	SPOOL

202	203	204	205	206
BEES ON A BASKET	THREE FRUITS	THREE FRUITS	POPPY	FLUTE

191 – $90; **192** – $150 (R); **193** – $45; **194** – $165 (R); **195** – $75; **196** – $75; **197** – $75; **198** – $80; **199** – $85 (S); **200** – $60; **201** – $65 (Atterbury); **202** – $55; **203** – $75; **204** – $65; **205** – $65; **206** – $50 (Fenton).

Panelled Poppies

207
PANELLED POPPIES

207 — $850 (S).

Custard Glass by

A. H. Heisey Glass Company

Newark, Ohio

207-A
PURITAN
(rare compote)

207-D
WINGED SCROLL
(rare bulbous salt)

207-B
WINGED SCROLL
(decorated ring tree)

207-C
BEADED PANEL & SUNBURST
(rare punch cup)

207A — $225 (VR); **207B** — $200 (R); **207C** — $120 (VR); **207D** — $150 (VR).

Winged Scroll

208 PITCHER (bulbous)	209 TUMBLER	210 PITCHER (tankard)	211 VASE	212 VASE	213 VASE

214 TOOTHPICK	215 SPOONER	216 BUTTER	217 SUGAR	218 CREAMER

219 HUMIDOR (lid missing)	220 CIGARETTE HOLDER	221 MATCH HOLDER	222 CELERY	223 SALT	224 SYRUP	225 PEPPER

208 – $225; **209** – $55; **210** – $200; **211** – $90; **212** – $75; **213** – $75; **214** – $85; **215** – $75; **216** – $150; **217** – $90; **218** – $75; **219** – $275 (w/lid); **220** – $165; **221** – $165; **222** – $275 (R); **223** – $65 (S); **224** – $200; **225** – $60 (S).

226
HIGH STANDARD
COMPOTE

227
CRUET

228
TRINKET BOX

224
COLOGNE

230
CAKE STAND

Winged Scroll

231
BON-BON

232
NAPPY

233
OLIVE DISH

234
PICKLE DISH

235
CUP & SAUCER

236
SAUCE

237
BERRY BOWL

238
MASTER BERRY

239
SAUCE

226 – $350; **227** – $185; **228** – $85; **229** – $225 (S); **230** – $300 (R); **231** – $45; **232** – $45; **233** – $45; **234** – $45; **235** – $145 (R); **236** – $35; **237** – $110; **238** – $130; **239** – $40.

Ring Band
(P)

240 CELERY VASE	241 TOOTHPICK	242 TUMBLER (variant)	243 TUMBLER	244 PITCHER	245 TUMBLER
246 SALT	247 PEPPER	248 SPOONER	249 BUTTER	250 SUGAR	251 CREAMER
252 SYRUP	253 JELLY	254 CRUET SET TRAY		255 CUSTARD	256 CRUET (n.o.s.)

240 – $235 (R); **241** – $75; **242** – $50; **243** – $60; **244** – $235; **245** – $55; **246** – $30; **247** – $30; **248** – $75; **249** – $170; **250** – $115; **251** – $75; **252** – $250 (S); **253** – $145; **254** – $165; **255** – $45; **256** – $195.

CUSTARD GLASS BY A. H. HEISEY

257 258
CUT BLOCK
indiv. sugar indiv. creamer

259
master
ice cream

RING BAND

260
indiv.
ice cream

261
WINGED SCROLL
dresser tray

262
PUNTY BAND
souv. creamer

263
PINEAPPLE & FAN
souvenir pitcher

264
BEADED PANEL & SUNBURST
2-piece punch bowl

265
PUNCH CUP
(signed)

266 267
BEAD SWAG
goblet wine

257 — $35; **258** — $35; **259** — $195 (R); **260** — $48 (S); **261** — $245; **262** — $32; **263** — $40; **264** — $1200 (VR); **265** — $45; **266** — $65; **267** — $75.

Winged Scroll Smoke Set

(Humidor, cigar holder & cigarette holder on tray)

268 — $100; 269 — $185 (S); 270 — $140; 271 — $275 (VR).

Custard Glass by
Tarentum Glass Company

Tarentum, Pa.

271-A
HEART WITH THUMBPRINT
(oil lamp)

271A — $200.

272
CRUET
(green opaque)

273
CRUET
(decorated)

274
CRUET
(o.s.)

275
TUMBLER

276
PITCHER

275
TUMBLER

277
SPOONER

278
TOOTHPICK

279
BUTTER

280
SUGAR

281
CREAMER

Georgia Gem
(P)

282
BREAKFAST
SUGAR

283
BREAKFAST
CREAMER

284
SALT

285
PEPPER

286
MASTER BERRY

287
SAUCE

272 – $165; **273** – $195 (S); **274** – $165; **275** – $42; **276** – $175; **277** – $48; **278** – $65; **279** – $135; **280** – $70; **281** – $50; **282** – $42; **283** – $38; **284** – $98 pr.; **285** – $98 pr.; **286** – $95; **287** – $25.

CUSTARD GLASS BY TARENTUM

Tarentum's
Victoria
(OMN)

Heart with
Thumbprint

| 288 PITCHER | 289 TUMBLER | 290 CELERY VASE | 291 FINGER LAMP | 292 WINE | 293 KEROSENE LAMP (large size) |

| 294 SUGAR | 295 SPOONER | 296 BUTTER | 297 CREAMER |

| 298 SALT | 299 SAUCE | 300 MASTER BERRY | 299 SAUCE |

288 – $325 (R); **289** – $75; **290** – $220 (S); **291** – $125; **292** – $85; **293** – $200 (R); **294** – $125 (S); **295** – $90 (S); **296** – $225 (R); **297** – $90 (S); **298** – $85 (R); **299** – $48; **300** – $175.

Cane Insert (K)

301 SAUCE	302 MASTER BERRY	303 SUGAR	304 SPOONER	305 PITCHER (green opaque)

Tarentum's Tiny Thumbprint (A)

306 SPOONER — 307 BUTTER — 308 SUGAR — 309 CREAMER — 310 TOOTHPICK — 311 SALT — 312 PEPPER

Panelled Teardrop (P)

313 SOUVENIR BUD VASE — 314 SOUV VASE (transfer decor.) — 315 SOUVENIR PITCHER — 316 SOUVENIR WINE — 317 CUSTARD — 318 SUGAR SHAKER

301 — $40; **302** — $125; **303** — $110; **304** — $80; **305** — $165; **306** — $75; **307** — $175 (S); **308** — $100 (S); **309** — $85; **310** — $90 (S); **311** — $95 pr. (R); **312** — $95 pr. (R); **313** — $24; **314** — $24; **315** — $28; **316** — $48; **317** — $35; **318** — $135.

Custard Glass by

Jefferson Glass Company

Follansbee, W. Va.

318-A
DIAMOND WITH PEG
(rare napkin ring)

318-B
salt

318-C
pepper

318-D
toothpick

318A — $135 (R); **318B** — $95 pr. (S); **318C** — $95 pr. (S); **318D** — $85 (R).

Ribbed Drape (G)

| 319 SALT | 320 CRUET (o.s.) | 321 PEPPER | 322 PITCHER | 323 TUMBLER | 324 JELLY |

| 325 SPOONER | 326 BUTTER | 327 CREAMER | 328 SUGAR | 329 TOOTHPICK |

Jefferson Optic (A)

| 330 SUGAR | 331 BUTTER | 332 SPOONER | 333 MASTER BERRY | 334 SAUCE | 335 TUMBLER |

319 — $185 pr. (VR); **320** — $300 (S); **321** — $165 pr. (VR); **322** — $310 (R); **323** — $60; **324** — $135 (R); **325** — $85; **326** — $225 (S); **327** — $85; **328** — $125 (S); **329** — $120; **330** — $95 (S); **331** — $135 (R); **332** — $70; **333** — $90; **334** — $28; **335** — $38.

Diamond with Peg (P)

| 336 TUMBLER | 337 PITCHER | 338 PITCHER | 339 PITCHER | 340 BUTTER |

| 341 MASTER BERRY | 342 SAUCE | 343 SALT | 344 PEPPER | 345 TOOTHPICK | 346 SHOT GLASS (souv.) | 347 CUSTARD (souv.) |

Ribbed Thumbprint (k)

| 348 TUMBLER | 349 SOUVENIR CREAMER | 350 INDIVIDUAL OPEN SUGAR | 351 INDIVIDUAL CREAMER | 352 TOOTHPICK | 353 MUG |

336 – $45; 337 – $250; 338 – $135; 339 – $110; 340 – $185; 341 – $100; 342 – $30; 343 – $30; 344 – $30; 345 – $45; 346 – $38; 347 – $40; 348 – $45; 349 – $35; 350 – $40; 351 – $38; 352 – $45; 353 – $35.

Cherry & Scale
(G)

354
BUTTER

355
TUMBLER

356
PITCHER

355
TUMBLER

357
SPOONER

358
SUGAR

359
MASTER
BERRY

360
SAUCE

361
HORSE
MEDALLIONS

362
STALKING
LION

363
DRAGON
& LOTUS

364
PERSIAN
MEDALLION

354 — $210; **355** — $50; **356** — $275 (S); **357** — $85; **358** — $125; **359** — $120; **360** — $35;
361 — $75; **362** — $80; **363** — $70; **364** — $65.

Vermont
(OMN)

365
VASE

366
PICKLE
TRAY

367
TUMBLER

368
PITCHER

369
WASTE
BOWL

370
SPOONER

371
BUTTER

372
SUGAR

373
CREAMER

374
TOOTHPICK

375
SALT

376
SMALL
CARD
TRAY

377
MEDIUM
CARD
TRAY

378
LARGE
CARD
TRAY

379
SAUCE

380
MASTER
BERRY

365 — $75; **366** — $48; **367** — $55; **368** — $235; **369** — $75 (R); **370** — $75; **371** — $175; **372** — $115; **373** — $75; **374** — $75; **375** — $60; **376** — $75; **377** — $90; **378** — $115; **379** — $35; **380** — $125.

Custard Souvenirs

381
WIDE BAND BELL

382
WIDE BAND BELL

383
SOUVENIR PLATE

384
ROWS OF RINGS VASE

385
PANEL BOTTOM VASE

386
SOUV. SHOT GLASS

387
RING & BEADS
(souv. creamer)

388
RING & BEADS

389
WHIMSEY MUG

390
WHIMSEY POT

391
WHIMSEY ALE

392
6-SIDED NAPKIN RING

393
McKEE HONEYCOMB
(wine)

394
DIAMOND WITH PEG
(wine)

395
JEFFERSON FLEUR-DE-LIS
(hair receiver)

396
GEORGIA GEM
(hair receiver)

397
WASHINGTON

398
SOUV. CUSTARD CUP

381 – $140; **382** – $140; **383** – $55; **384** – $40; **385** – $35; **386** – $22; **387** – $22; **388** – $35; **389** – $25; **390** – $38; **391** – $26; **392** – $85 (S); **393** – $75; **394** – $75; **395** – $55; **396** – $55; **397** – $48; **398** – $38.

Miscellaneous Custard Glass

(including lamps,"late" custard & miscellaneous additions)

398A – $750; **398B** – $65 pr.; **398C** – $500; **398D** – $30; **398E** – $45.

399
GEORGIA GEM
(celery)

400
HARVARD
(wine)

401
RIBBED THUMBPRINT
(wine)

402
SOUV. SALT
(tall)

403
JEFFERSON OPTIC
(cruet)

404
PANEL BOTTOM VASE
(no sour.)

405
WINGED SCROLL
(ash tray)

406
salt
LEAF COVERED BASE

407
pepper

408
JEWELLED VERMONT
(candlestick)

409
SAUCE

Delaware
(Figures 409-414)

410
TUMBLER

411
BREAKFAST SUGAR
(open)

412
BREAKFAST CREAMER

413
PIN TRAY

414
RING TRAY

399 − $170; **400** − $75; **401** − $75; **402** − $35; **403** − $175 (S); **404** − $45; **405** − $125 (S); **406** − $48 pr.; **407** − $48 pr.; **408** − $50; **409** − $48; **410** − $48; **411** − $65; **412** − $55; **413** − $50; **414** − $65.

Tan

415
TRUMPET
VASE

416
INDIVIDUAL
ICE CREAM

417
MASTER
ICE CREAM

418
PLATE
(Cambridge)

419
CREASED BALE
(syrup)

420
SMOCKING
(bell)

421
SERENADE
MUG

422
PANELLED CANE
(souv. pitcher)

423
DAISY BAND
(shade)

424
FLORA
SCROLL
(puff box)

425
SPIDER WEB
(Alba variant)

426
RING & BEADS
(souv. toothpick)

427
RING & BEADS
(decor. t.p.)

428
SUNSET
(salt & pepper)

429

430
LITTLE
COLUMNS
(salt)

431
TINY THUMB-
PRINT
(toothpick)

432
PANELLED
TEARDROP
(salt)

433
HARVARD

415 – $75; **416** – $50 (S); **417** – $200 (R); **418** – $50; **419** – $160 (S); **420** – $50 (Akro);
421 – $55 (McKee); **422** – $45 (Heisey); **423** – $45; **424** – $65; **425** – $32; **426** – $28;
427 – $75 (R); **428** – $30; **429** – $30; **430** – $28; **431** – $45; **432** – $60 (S); **433** – $50.

434
SILVER OVERLAY
(Cambridge)

435
TROUBADOUR
(goblet)

436
VERMONT
(celery vase)

437
HEART WITH
THUMBPRINT
(med. lamp)

438
BEADED
CIRCLE
(jelly)

439
BEADED
SWAG
(pickle)

440
BEADED
CIRCLE
(tumbler)

441
SINGING
BIRDS
(mug)

442
RARE
POLITICAL
commemorative

443
HEART
(salt)

444
GENEVA
(rust decor.)

445
HEART WITH
THUMBPRINT
(open sugar)

446
LIBBEY'S
MAIZE
(ivory t.p.)

447
TINY
SAWTOOTH
(mini. lamp base)

434 – $135 (S); **435** – $75 (S); **436** – $200 (S); **437** – $175; **438** – $245 (R); **439** – $250 (VR); **440** – $75 (R); **441** – $75; **442** – $95 (R); **443** – $30; **444** – $50 (S); **445** – $65; **446** – $245; **447** – $50.

448
NORTHWOOD
BLACKBERRY

449
MELON RIB
(mini. lamp base)

450
CROCODILE
TEARS
(mini. lamp)

451
NINE-PANEL
(mini. lamp base)

452
PEACOCK AT
THE FOUNTAIN
(tumbler)

453
NORTHWOOD GRAPE
(puff jar)

454
SAILBOAT
&
WINDMILL

455
LOUIS XV
(blue decor)

456
LOW SCROLL
(pin tray)

457
LOW SCROLL
(ring tree)

458
BLUEBIRDS

459
GRAPE FRIEZE

460
PRAYER RUG

448 – $40 (Fenton); **449** – $55; **450** – $220; **451** – $55; **452** – $75 (R); **453** – $195 (w/lid); **454** – $55; **455** – $115; **456** – $50; **457** – $120; **458** – $85 (Fenton); **459** – $195 (R); **460** – $25 (Fenton).

461
FOOTED WREATH
(bowl)

462
SUNSET
(lamp base)

463
CHRYSANTHEMUM
TRAY
(B)

464
SUNFLOWER
SCROLL
(nappy)

465 466
TORCH &
WREATH
(salt pepper)

467
BULGING
TEARDROP
(condiment set)

468
WOVEN
CANE
(salt)

469
DITHRIDGE
PRINCESS SWIRL
(condiment set)

470
HEART
(t.p.)

471
CREASED
BALE
(condiment set)

442 473
CORN
(salt pepper)

Trailing Vine

474 475
MASTER BERRY
&
SAUCE

476
COVERED
BUTTER

477
SPOONER

478
CREAMER

461 – $75; **462** – $125; **463** – $150 (McKee); **464** – $45; **465** – $55 pr.; **466** – $55 pr.;
467 – $135; **468** – $30; **469** – $165; **470** – $75; **471** – $165; **472** – $75 pr.; **473** – $75 pr.;
474 – $100; **475** – $35; **476** – $145; **477** – $65; **478** – $65.

479
(candlestick)

480
RAM'S HEAD
(bowl)

481

482
(COMPOTE)

483
McKEE'S
HONEYCOMB

484
FIGURAL FLOWER
HOLDER

485
SHAVING
VESSEL

486
ALE GLASS

487
DONUT STAND

488
ROLLING PIN

479 – $55; **480** – $225; **481** – $55; **482** – $95; **483** – $95; **484** – $350; **485** – $65;
486 – $45; **487** – $85; **488** – $125 (S).

489
ENGLISH VASE
(applied rigaree)

490
ELK DECORATED ALE

491
MT. WASHINGTON
(cracker jar)

492
SUNSET
(syrup)

493
SAILBOAT & WINDMILL
(decor. compote)

494
DOUBLE FAN BAND
(syrup)

495
FANTASIA
(salt)

496
RIB TWIST
(salt)

497
SAWTOOTH
(salt)

498
PANELLED 4-DOT
(salt)

489 — $160; **490** — $65 (S); **491** — $400 (R); **492** — $165; **493** — $60; **494** — $175 (R); **495** — $32; **496** — $32; **497** — $24; **498** — $32.

Encyclopedia of
Victorian Colored Pattern Glass
Book 5
U. S. Glass From A to Z

William Heacock & Fred Bickenheuser

A History of The Early Production Years of
THE UNITED STATES GLASS COMPANY

Bullseye & Fan

1   2   3   4

U.S. Glass In Color

(Includes patterns made by member factories)

4A   4B   4C

4D   4E   4F   4G

1 – $100; **2** – $60; **3** – $45; **4** – $80; **4A** – $135; **4B** – $35; **4C** – $200 (VR); **4D** – $225 (R); **4E** – $32; **4F** – $48; **4G** – $75.

5	6	5	7	8
TUMBLER	TANKARD	TUMBLER	PITCHER	PIN TRAY

Delaware

9	10	11	12	13
TOOTHPICK	SUGAR	CREAMER	SPOONER	BUTTER

Bohemian

14	15	16	17	18
TOOTHPICK	SUGAR	CREAMER	SPOONER	BUTTER

5 – $40; **6** – $175; **7** – $175; **8** – $65 (R); **9** – $100; **10** – $95; **11** – $60; **12** – $70; **13** – $145; **14** – $100 (S); **15** – $95; **16** – $55; **17** – $75; **18** – $145.

Michigan

| 19 SPOONER | 20 BUTTER | 21 SUGAR | 22 CREAMER | 23 PITCHER | 24 TUMBLER |

| 25 BUTTER | 26 SUGAR | 27 CREAMER | 28 SPOONER | 29 CRUET |

New Hampshire

| 30 GOBLET | 31 WINE | 32 CUSTARD | 33 TOOTHPICK | 34 SALT | 35 BREAKFAST SUGAR | 36 BREAKFAST CREAMER |

19 — $45; 20 — $100; 21 — $75; 22 — $45; 23 — $135; 24 — $32; 25 — $100; 26 — $75; 27 — $40; 28 — $45; 29 — $95 (S); 30 — $45; 31 — $45; 32 — $22; 33 — $35; 34 — $22; 35 — $25; 36 — $22.

37
Wooden Pail
WATER PITCHER

38
COMPOTE

39
TUMBLER

40
PITCHER

41
VASE

Colorado

42
CELERY

43
TUMBLER

44
WINE

45
IND. SUGAR

46
IND. CREAMER

47
Maine

48
SPOONER

49
SUGAR

50
BUTTER

51
CREAMER

Colorado

37 — $110; **38** — $125 (S); **39** — $35; **40** — $185 (S); **41** — $65; **42** — $110; **43** — $35; **44** — $35; **45** — $32; **46** — $30; **47** — $65; **48** — $50; **49** — $95; **50** — $135; **51** — $48.

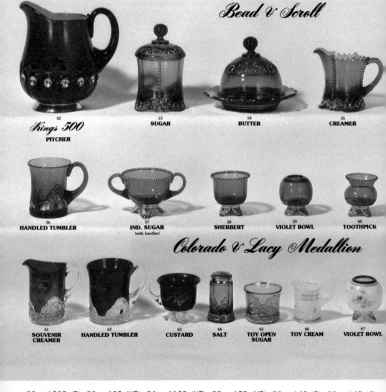

Bead & Scroll

52 *Kings 500* **PITCHER**	53 **SUGAR**	54 **BUTTER**	55 **CREAMER**

56 **HANDLED TUMBLER**	57 **IND. SUGAR** (with handles)	58 **SHERBERT**	59 **VIOLET BOWL**	60 **TOOTHPICK**

Colorado & Lacy Medallion

61 **SOUVENIR CREAMER**	62 **HANDLED TUMBLER**	63 **CUSTARD**	64 **SALT**	65 **TOY OPEN SUGAR**	66 **TOY CREAM**	67 **VIOLET BOWL**

52 – $225 (R); **53** – $90 (VR); **54** – $135 (VR); **55** – $70 (VR); **56** – $48 (R); **57** – $45 (S); **58** – $50; **59** – $45; **60** – $65; **61** – $30; **62** – $30; **63** – $24; **64** – $20; **65** – $22; **66** – $18; **67** – $32.

| 68 GOBLET | 69 PITCHER | 70 SALT | 71 SYRUP | 70 PEPPER | 72 *Long Loops* VASE |

Florida

| 73 MASTER BERRY | 74 IND. BERRY | 75 CRUET | 76 | 77 |
| | | | BREAKFAST SUGAR & CREAMER |

U. S. Rib

| 78 SUGAR | 79 BUTTER | 80 SPOONER | 81 CREAMER |

68 – $38; **69** – $70; **70** – $55 pr. (S); **71** – $200 (VR); **72** – $18; **73** – $35; **74** – $15; **75** – $90; **76** – $35; **77** – $30; **78** – $45; **79** – $90; **80** – $40; **81** – $40.

California
(Beaded Grape)

82 **CREAMER**	83 **SUGAR**	84 **BUTTER**	85 **SPOONER**	86 **WINE**	87 **PITCHER**

88 **SUGAR**	89 **CREAMER**	90 **BUTTER**	91 **SPOONER**

Daisy & Button with Crossbars

92 **SYRUP**	93 **GOBLET**	94 **CRUET**	95 **KETCHUP**	96 *Thousand Eye* (cruet set)

82 — $45; **83** — $65; **84** — $100; **85** — $60; **86** — $65 (R); **87** — $155 (S); **88** — $60; **89** — $38;
90 — $95; **91** — $48; **92** — $150; **93** — $38; **94** — $85; **95** — $85; **96** — $200.

97	98
Bohemian Grape	
JUICE TUMBLER & TANKARD	

U.S. Colonial
99
WINE

California
100
CAKE STAND

Dbl. Dahlia W. Lens
101
WINE

Illinois
102
PITCHER

Wildflower
103
PITCHER

Hanover
104
BUTTER

LEMONADE PITCHER
105

TUMBLER
106

WATER PITCHER
107

Bullseye & Fan

97 — $28 (S); **98** — $135 (R); **99** — $22; **100** — $75; **101** — $40; **102** — $165 (R); **103** — $100; **104** — $75 (S); **105** — $160; **106** — $38; **107** — $145.

108
D & B With Thumbprint
CELERY

109
Wheat & Barley
SYRUP

110
GOBLET

111
PITCHER

Spirea Band

110
GOBLET

112
BUTTER

113
SPOONER

114
SUGAR

115
CREAMER

Medallion

116
CREAMER

117
SUGAR

118
BUTTER

119
SPOONER

Finecut

*Possible U.S. Glass Patterns

108 – $65; **109** – $150 (S); **110** – $38; **111** – $85; **112** – $85; **113** – $45; **114** – $60; **115** – $40; **116** – $35; **117** – $60; **118** – $90; **119** – $45.

120	121	122	123	124
Palm Beach	*Finecut*	*Willow Oak*	*Spirea Band*	*Medallion*
PITCHER	GOBLET	GOBLET	GOBLET	PITCHER

125	126	127	128	129
Leaf & Flower	*Maine*	*Bryce Panel*	*Kings 500*	*Kings 500*
CELERY	SYRUP	SYRUP	SYRUP	CRUET

130	131	132	133	134
Thousand Eye	*Wooden Pail*	*Heavy Finecut*	*Three Panel*	
THREE-KNOB	SPOONER	SPOONER	SUGAR	CREAMER

120 – $300 (S); **121** – $40; **122** – $35; **123** – $38; **124** – $90; **125** – $65; **126** – $195 (R); **127** – $90; **128** – $200 (S); **129** – $135; **130** – $35; **131** – $35; **132** – $35; **133** – $60; **134** – $45.

Pattee Cross
PITCHER & TUMBLERS

135

136

Ruby Thumbprint

137
Panelled Palm
BUTTER

138
SUGAR

139
CREAMER

140
Colorado
PERFUME

141
Star-in-Bullseye

142
Mirror & Fan

143
Kentucky

144
Paeonia

145
Thousand Eye

120 — $300 (S); 121 — $40; 122 — $35; 123 — $38; 124 — $90; 125 — $65; 126 — $195 (R);
127 — $90; 128 — $200 (S); 129 — $135; 130 — $35; 131 — $35; 132 — $35; 133 — $60;
134 — $45.

60

146
Barred Oval
PITCHER

147
Bullseye & Daisy
SPOONER

148
BUTTER

149
VASE

Virginia

150
SUGAR

151
BUTTER

152
CREAMER

Colorado

153
SPOONER

154
BUTTER

155
SUGAR

156
CREAMER

Wooden Pail

146 – $145 (S); **147** – $50 (S); **148** – $120 (S); **149** – $65; **150** – $110; **151** – $160;
152 – $75; **153** – $48; **154** – $100 (R); **155** – $75 (R); **156** – $40.

157
Tiny Finecut
WINE DECANTER

158
Panelled Dogwood

159
Bohemian
COLOGNE

160
Delaware
CELERY

161

162
Beaded Swirl
PITCHER & TUMBLERS

161

163
U.S. Sheraton
NIGHT LAMP

164

165
Panelled Dogwood
BERRY BOWL & SAUCES

164

157 — $95; 158 — $120; 159 — $100; 160 — $85; 161 — $22; 162 — $95; 163 — $65 (S); 164 — $24; 165 — $55.

166 Bohemian STRAW JAR

167 Bullseye & Fan LEMONADE

168 Bearded Man

NOT U.S. GLASS

169 Maine MILK PITCHER

170 Pavonia CELERY

171

172 Late Block WATER SET

173 SUGAR

174 CREAMER

175 SPOONER

176 BUTTER

177 Two Panel MASTER & INDIV. SALT

178

Double-Eye Hobnail

166 — $150 (R); 167 — $120; 168 — $120 (VR); 169 — $85; 170 — $60 (S); 171 — $30;
172 — $145; 173 — $75 (S); 174 — $45 (S); 175 — $55 (S); 176 — $95 (S); 177 — $18;
178 — $28.

Broken Column

| 179 SAUCE | 180 COV. COMPOTE | 181 NAPPY | 182 BUTTER | 183 TUMBLER | 184 PITCHER | 183 TUMBLER |

Daisy & Button
(with Red Dots)

| 185 TUMBLER | 186 PITCHER | 185 TUMBLER | 187 TOOTHPICK | 188 SHOE | 189 WALL RECEPTICLE |

| 190 Duncan Block SYRUP | 191 Saxon SYRUP | 192 SPOONER | 193 BUTTER | 194 SUGAR | 195 CREAMER |

Crystal Wedding

179 — $22; **180** — $275 (VR); **181** — $28; **182** — $140; **183** — $50; **184** — $175; **185** — $35; **186** — $165 (R); **187** — $50; **188** — $52 (S); **189** — $48 (S); **190** — $145 (R); **191** — $135 (S); **192** — $50; **193** — $120; **194** — $85; **195** — $45.

196 TUMBLER   **197 BULBOUS PITCHER**   **196 TUMBLER**   **198 TUMBLER**   **199**   **198 TUMBLER**

Ruby Thumbprint

(Figures 196-197, 200-203)

Washington

200 BUTTER   **201 CUP & SAUCER**   **202 MILK PITCHER**   **203 GOBLET**

204 *Snail* CRUET   **205 *Dakota* WINE**   **206 *Peas & Pods* WINE**   **207 *Bevelled Diamond & Star* WINE**   **208 *Washington* CORDIAL**

196 — $32; **197** — $145; **198** — $28; **199** — $130; **200** — $110; **201** — $55; **202** — $110; **203** — $48; **204** — $175 (VR); **205** — Heisey's ''Punty Band''; **206** — $32 (R); **207** — $30; **208** — $35 (S).

209 Bullseye & Daisy   210 Arched Ovals   211 Pennsylvania   212 Two Panel   213 Finecut & Panel   214 Cathedral

215 Tiny Finecut   216 Ruby Thumbprint   217 Kings Crown   218 Washington   219 Roanoke   220 New Jersey

221 Millard   222 Star-in-Bullseye   223 Minnesota   224 Pennsylvania   225 Bullseye & Fan

209 – $32; **210** – $22; **211** – $32; **212** – $36; **213** – $28; **214** – $38; **215** – $28; **216** – $24; **217** – $35; **218** – $35 (S); **219** – $28; **220** – $40 (S); **221** – $65; **222** – $50; **223** – $75 (R); **224** – $32; **225** – $75 (R).

U.S. Glass Cruets

226	227	228	229	230
U.S. Colonial	Shoshone	U.S. Rib	Delaware	Beaded Swirl

231	232	233	234	235
Amazon	D & B With Crossbar	Panelled D & B (Amberette)	Millard N.O.S.	Millard N.O.S.

236	237	238	239
Virginia	Saxon	Pennsylvania	Nail

226 — $55; **227** — $75; **228** — $75; **229** — $150 (S); **230** — $90; **231** — $110; **232** — $100; **233** — $165 (S); **234** — $80; **235** — $80; **236** — $110; **237** — $85; **238** — $110 (S); **239** — $150 (R).

240 — Diamond Bridges   241 — Berkeley   242 — Nail   243 — Cathedral   244 — Bead & Scroll

245 — Moon & Star   246   247 — Zippered Swirl & Diamond   248 — Pleating   249

250 — Roanoke   251 — O'Hara Diamond   252 — Scalloped Swirl   253 — Cottage

240 — $75 (R); **241** — $135 (S); **242** — $48 (S); **243** — $42; **244** — $65; **245** — $95 (R); **246** — $75 (R); **247** — $75 (S); **248** — $48; **249** — $65; **250** — $32 (S); **251** — $120; **252** — $24; **253** — $38.

254 Beaded Block (cruet)

255 Bohemian (celery)

256 Michigan (celery)

257 D & B With Thumbprint (butter)

258 Majestic Crown (sugar)

259 Hobnail w. Thumbprint (toy set)

260 (cruet)

261

262 Manhattan (syrup)

263

264 Hobb's Hobnail (toy water set)

(salt)

265 Silver Queen

266 Triple Triangle

267 Finecut & Block

268 New York (wines and cordials)

269 Log & Star

270 Prism & Daisy Bar

271 Doyle's Shell

254 — $95 (S); 255 — $85; 256 — $85; 257 — $110; 258 — $120; 259 — $225 set; 260 — $85 (S); 261 — $55 pr.; 262 — $165 (R); 263 — $45; 264 — $175 (S); 265 — $28 (S); 266 — $32; 267 — $55 (R); 268 — $45, 269 — $55 (R); 270 — $32; 271 — $32.

1000
Toothpick Holders

A Collector's Guide

by

william heacock

Sponsored By The National Toothpick Holder Collectors' Society

Late Additions

851
PIG ON BOX CAR

852
LEAF AND STAR

853
FLEUR-DE-LIS

854
RIB-BASE
HOBNAIL

855
DAUM NANCY

856
DAUM NANCY

857
JEWELLED
HEART

858
LEAF
UMBRELLA

859
BUBBLE LATTICE

860
RED SLAG

861
THORNY TREE
TRUNK

862
STAR-IN-
SQUARE

863
THREADED HAT

864
NEVADA

865
RINGS
AND BEADS

866
DOUBLE-RING
PANEL

867
BOHEMIAN

868
PLAIN BAND

851 – $110 (R); **852** – $85 (VR); **853** – $55 (S); **854** – $32 (S); **855** – $275 (R); **856** – $300 (VR); **857** – $85 (S); **858** – $85 (S); **859** – $125 (VR); **860** – $65; **861** – $55; **862** – $95 (R); **863** – $28; **864** – $55 (S); **865** – $28; **866** – $40 (S); **867** – $75 (S); **868** – $35.

Art Glass

1 BURMESE	**2** BURMESE	**3** BURMESE	**4** BURMESE	**5** BURMESE

6 PEACHBLOW	**7** PEACHBLOW	**8** PEACHBLOW	**9** PEACHBLOW	**10** AGATA

11 DAISY & BUTTON AMBERINA	**12** DAISY & BUTTON AMBERINA	**13** AMBERINA	**14** AMBERINA

15 AMBERINA	**16** AMBERINA	**17** AMBERINA	**18** REVERSE AMBERINA	**19** WHEELING PEACHBLOW

1 — $400 (R); **2** — $425 (VR); **3** — $350 (R); **4** — $275 (S); **5** — $350 (S); **6** — $375; **7** — $425;
8 — $400; **9** — $450; **10** — $450 (S); **11** — $175 (VR); **12** — $150; **13** — $350 (VR); **14** — $175;
15 — $150; **16** — $160; **17** — $150; **18** — $120 (R); **19** — $325 (S).

Art Glass

20
MT. WASHINGTON
BROWNIE

21
PAIRPOINT
BUFFALO

22
SWIRLED
TINY FINGERS

23
FIG MOLD

24
SWIRLED
SQUARE-TOP

25
CROWN MILANO

26
WEBB BURMESE

27
BURMESE

28
BURMESE

29
BURMESE

30
CROWN MILANO

31
SMITH
BROTHERS

32
WAVECREST

33
PARALLEL
GREEK KEY

34
FIG MOLD

35
RAINBOW
MOTHER-OF-PEARL

36
DAUM
NANCY

37
TIFFANY

38
AMBERINA

39
AMBERINA

20 — $400 (VR); **21** — $75; **22** — $450 (VR); **23** — $375 (R); **24** — $120; **25** — $120; **26** — $350 (S); **27** — $250 (S); **28** — $225; **29** — $225; **30** — $150; **31** — $85; **32** — $75; **33** — $175 (R); **34** — $195 (S); **35** — $750 (VR); **36** — $175 (S); **37** — $175; **38** — $225 (S); **39** — $185.

Art Glass

40
CROWN MILANO

41
SWIRLED
BEAD-TOP

42
SWIRLED
BEAD-TOP

43
FIG MOLD
BURMESE

44
BURMESE

45
ONYX

46
ROSE ONYX

47
GLOSSY
BURMESE

48
GLOSSY
BURMESE

49
BURMESE

50
AGATA

51
CORALENE

52
POMONA

53
ROSE QUILT

54
PEACHBLOW

55
DAUM NANCY

56
TIFFANY

57
LIBBEY'S
LITTLE LOBE

58
PARALLEL
GREEK KEY

59
SIMPLE
SCROLL

40 – $260 (VR); **41** – $100; **42** – $195 (S); **43** – $400 (VR); **44** – $400 (R); **45** – $350;
46 – $475 (R); **47** – $350 (R); **48** – $425 (VR); **49** – $275 (S); **50** – $400 (S); **51** – $300 (R);
52 – $200; **53** – $150; **54** – $350; **55** – $150; **56** – $125; **57** – $85; **58** – $125; **59** – $85.

60
AMBER-RIM
OVERLAY

61
M.W.
LUSTERLESS WHITE

62
M.W.
SATIN HAT

63
DIAMOND QUILT
BURMESE

64
PAIRPOINT
POINTER

65
FIG MOLD

66
LITTLE LOBE

67
PARALLEL
GREEK KEY

68
POMONA

69
POMONA

70
POMONA

71
PSEUDO POMONA

72
BRITISH
BARREL

73
RAINBOW
TWISTER

74
IRIDESCENT
URN

75
STEUBEN
AURENE

76
TIFFANY

77
INVERTED
THUMBPRINT

60 – $95; **61** – $60; **62** – $135; **63** – $350; **64** – $75; **65** – $150; **66** – $75; **67** – $195 (S);
68 – $175; **69** – $120; **70** – $120; **71** – $95 (R); **72** – $75; **73** – $125 (R); **74** – $125 (S);
75 – $150; **76** – $200; **77** – $45.

78 MOTHER-OF-PEARL	**79** CORALENE	**80** BURMESE	**81** AMBER-RIM OVERLAY

82
PAIRPOINT
PONY

83
KELVA
TYPE

84
WAVECREST

85
WAVECREST

86
EASTER
EGG

87
FREE-FORM
HOBNAIL

88
FIG MOLD

89
PARALLEL
GREEK KEY

90
POMONA

91
SIMPLE SCROLL

92
LABELLE
OPAL

93
HOOPED
BARREL

94
HOOPED
BARREL

95
LIBBEY
MAIZE

96
THREADED
CRYSTAL

78 — $250 (R); **79** — $250 (S); **80** — $295; **81** — $125; **82** — $95; **83** — $165 (S); **84** — $130; **85** — $165; **86** — $75; **87** — $85 (S); **88** — $195; **89** — $200 (S); **90** — $200; **91** — $85; **92** — $50; **93** — $45; **94** — $45; **95** — $250 (S); **96** — $60.

Art & Colored Glass

97
WEBB
MOTHER-OF-PEARL

98
FLORA

99
BEES ON A
BASKET

100
RIBBED DRAPE

101
MINNESOTA

102
ALEXANDRITE

103
RING BASE
AMBERINA

104
LOUIS XV

105
WILD ROSE
WITH BOWKNOT

106
BEAD SWAG

107
JEWELLED
HEART

108
JEWELLED
HEART

109
HOBNAIL
BY HOBBS

110
DOUBLE EYE
HOBNAIL

111
MEDALLION
SPRIG

112
TACOMA

113
QUARTERED
BLOCK

114
SUNBEAM

115
CHAMPION

116
SHOESHONE

97 – $235; **98** – $250 (VR); **99** – $75; **100** – $70 (S); **101** – $75 (R); **102** – $1250 (VR); **103** – $200 (R); **104** – $750 (VR); **105** – $120 (R); **106** – $85; **107** – $175 (R); **108** – $225 (VR); **109** – $175 (VR); **110** – $50; **111** – $135 (S); **112** – $75; **113** – $60 (S); **114** – $65 (R); **115** – $55; **116** – $75 (S).

Art & Colored Glass

117
LEANING OVERLAY

118
JACK-IN-
THE-PULPIT

119
CURTAIN TOP
OVERLAY

120
RIBBON
OVERLAY

121
RUFFLE-TOP
OVERLAY

122
DECORATED
RUBINA

123
VENECIA

124
BULGE-BASE
RUBINA

125
BLOWN
HERRINGBONE

126
SPATTER

127
PALM LEAF

128
GUTTATE

129
PINE APPLE

130
FLORETTE

131
CROCODILE
TEARS

132
DECORATED
RUBINA

133
DECORATED
CRANBERRY

134
REVERSE SWIRL
SPECKLED

135
OPTIC
THUMBPRINT

136
COLORADO

117 – $90; **118** – $75; **119** – $75; **120** – $85; **121** – $85; **122** – $200 (S); **123** – $75; **124** – $60; **125** – $60; **126** – $45; **127** – $65; **128** – $60; **129** – $55; **130** – $55; **131** – $75 (S); **132** – $85; **133** – $75; **134** – $100; **135** – $65; **136** – $55 (S).

Art & Colored Glass

137
VENECIA

138
JEFFERSON OPTIC

139
JEFFERSON OPTIC

140
POMONA

141
POMONA

142
SKIRTED OPTIC

143
RING BASE

144
TALL & SKINNY

145
SHORT & DUMPY

146
DUCK-FOOT

147
DECORATED BLUINA IVT

148
BLUINA IVT

149
PEACH OPAL DIAMOND

150
CHRYSANTHEMUM BASE SPECKLED

151
LEAF MOLD

152
INTAGLIO DAISY

153
INTAGLIO SUNFLOWER

154
DUCHESS

155
HOBNAIL BY HOBBS

156
APPLE & GRAPE IN SCROLL

137 – $60; **138** – $45; **139** – $50; **140** – $135; **141** – $165 (S); **142** – $40; **143** – $75; **144** – $45; **145** – $35; **146** – $40; **147** – $135 (S); **148** – $85 (S); **149** – $100 (S); **150** – $85 (R); **151** – $100 (VR); **152** – $40; **153** – $40; **154** – $100 (S); **155** – $45; **156** – $100 (R).

Colored Pattern Glass

157
PUNTY BAND

158
PUNTY BAND

159
TINY THUMBPRINT

160
JEFFERSON OPTIC

161
RING & BEADS

162
BEAD SWAG

163
WINGED SCROLL

164
BULGING LOOPS

165
ONE-O-ONE

166
AUSTRIAN

167
BUBBLE LATTICE

168
REVERSE SWIRL
(collared)

169
WINGED SCROLL

170
IRIS WITH MEANDER

171
IDYLL

172
INVERTED FAN & FEATHER
(repro)

173
(old)

174
PINE APPLE

175
CONE

176
BULGING LOOPS

157 — $50; **158** — $50; **159** — $55; **160** — $95 (R); **161** — $85 (S); **162** — $150 (S); **163** — $225 (R); **164** — $125 (R); **165** — $75; **166** — $150 (S); **167** — $100 (S); **168** — $65; **169** — $400 (VR); **170** — $48; **171** — $95 (R); **172** — repro; **173** — $550 (S); **174** — $85 (S); **175** — $95 (S); **176** — $75.

Colored Pattern Glass

177
PENNSYLVANIA

178
BULLSEYE AND
BUTTON

179
FANCY LOOP

180
GEORGIA GEM

181
BULLSEYE & FAN

182
HEART BAND

183
BEADED OVALS
IN SAND

184
NESTOR

185
INSIDE RIBBING

186
LINED LONG
PANELS

187
DAISY
ROSETTE

188
DAISY
ROSETTE

189
DAISY
ROSETTE

190
COINSPOT
(pedestalled)

191
NESTOR

192
JEFFERSON
OPTIC

193
ROYAL IVY

194
PANELLED
SPRIG

195
VENECIA

196
LADY ANNE

177 — $40; **178** — $95 (VR); **179** — $65; **180** — $65; **181** — $95 (R); **182** — $50 (S); **183** — $75;
184 — $85; **185** — $55; **186** — $60; **187** — $38; **188** — $38; **189** — $38; **190** — $65; **191** — $75;
192 — $55; **193** — $120; **194** — $95 (S); **195** — $75; **196** — $55.

Colored Pattern Glass

197
TREE OF LIFE

198
PICKET

199
TAPERED
BLOCK

200
COLORADO

201
DIAMOND POINT
AND LEAF

202
FLORETTE

203
FLORETTE

204
SWIRL AND
LEAF

205
HOBNAIL
By Hobbs

206
PEBBLE BAND

207
RING & BEADS

208
TINY
THUMBPRINT

209
GALLOWAY

210
BUTTON ARCHES

211
DAISY & BUTTON

212
MODEL PEERLESS

213
FLUTE

197 — $55; **198** — $65 (S); **199** — $35; **200** — $35; **201** — $45; **202** — $85 (VR); **203** — $50; **204** — $55; **205** — $45 (S); **206** — $48; **207** — $75; **208** — $30; **209** — $65 (R); **210** — $30; **211** — $35; **212** — $65 (R); **213** — $65 (S).

Color–Stained Glass

214
DUCHESS

215
STAR-IN-BULLSEYE

216
LADDER WITH DIAMOND

217
NEW HAMPSHIRE

218
VICTORIA
(Riverside's)

219
PILLOW AND SUNBURST

220
DUNCAN #42

221
PLEATING

222
BUTTON ARCHES

223
ATLAS

224
DOUGLASS

225
SAXON

226
ZIPPER SLASH

227
HALL OF MIRRORS

228
LOCKET ON CHAIN

229
VICTORIA
(Riverside's)

230
BRITTANIC

231
MILLARD

232
TACOMA

233
ZIPPER SLASH

214 – $60 (S); **215** – $40; **216** – $75 (R); **217** – $55 (R); **218** – $120 (R); **219** – $75 (S); **220** – $75 (S); **221** – $45; **222** – $30; **223** – $40; **224** – $50 (R); **225** – $35; **226** – $30; **227** – $35; **228** – $550 (VR); **229** – $100 (S); **230** – $65; **231** – $60; **232** – $65; **233** – $55.

Color-Stained Glass

234
FLOWER WITH CANE

235
TROPHY

236
ELEPHANT TOES

237
MICHIGAN

238
PANELLED PALM

239
ESTHER
(etched)

240
DIAMOND POINT SKIRT

241
ZIPPERED SWIRL AND DIAMOND

242
CZARINA

243
FANCY LOOP

244
LENOX

245
PLAIN BAND

246
TARENTUM THUMBPRINT

247
STAR BANNER

248
TRIUMPH

249
DAISY & BUTTON

250
ROYAL CRYSTAL

251
SWINGER

252
KING'S ROYAL

253
CO-OP'S ROYAL

234 – $35; **235** – $25; **236** – $35; **237** – $45; **238** – $45 (S); **239** – $60; **240** – $45; **241** – $55 (S); **242** – $45; **243** – $85 (R); **244** – $80 (VR); **245** – $40; **246** – $45; **247** – $35; **248** – $35; **249** – $95 (VR); **250** – $95 (VR); **251** – $22; **252** – $25; **253** – $35.

lored Pattern Glass (Toothpicks & Toy Spooners)

254
HOBNAIL WITH
THUMBPRINT BASE

255
HOBNAIL WITH
THUMBPRINT BASE

256
MENAGERIE

257
TWIST

258
DUTCH
KIDS

259
MICHIGAN

260
MICHIGAN

261
STIPPLED DEWDROP
AND RAINDROP

262
STIPPLED VINES
AND BEADS

263
TAPPAN

264
FROSTED
LION

265
KITTENS

286
CACTUS
(old)

267
CACTUS
(new)

268
TOLTEC

269
BULGING LOOPS

270
LEAF
UMBRELLA

271
LEAF
UMBRELLA

272
SPEARPOINT
BAND

254 – $38; **255** – $45; **256** – $55; **257** – $65; **258** – $65; **259** – $45; **260** – $75 (S);
261 – $75 (VR); **262** – $75 (VR); **263** – $20; **264** – $75; **265** – $120; **266** – $58; **267** – (repro);
268 – $40; **269** – $55; **270** – $75; **271** – $85; **272** – $30.

Art & Colored Glass

| 273 DIAMOND PANELS | 274 DIAMOND PANELS | 275 CAMBRIDGE COLONIAL | 276 CAMBRIDGE COLONIAL | 277 CAMBRIDGE SNOWFLAKE |

| 278 JEFFERSON COLONIAL | 279 PENNSYLVANIA | 280 SPRING MEADOWS | 281 ROSE PETAL WHIMSEY | 282 CORALENE (Bristol) |

| 283 LEANING OVERLAY | 284 WILD ROSE WITH BOWKNOT | 285 SPATTER SPIRAL | 286 TORTOISE SHELL (bulge base) | 287 TORTOISE SHELL (ring base) |

| 288 SAWTOOTHED HONEYCOMB | 289 SKIRT TOP OVERLAY | 290 LAZY AMBERINA | 291 WICKER BASKET | 292 WICKER BASKET |

273 – $35; **274** – $35; **275** – $30; **276** – $30; **277** – $35; **278** – $35; **279** – $75 (R); **280** – $55; **281** – $95 (S); **282** – $85; **283** – $80; **284** – $95; **285** – $75; **286** – $55; **287** – $55; **288** – $60 (S); **289** – $65; **290** – $75; **291** – $40; **292** – $40.

Assorted Colored Glass

(Pattern & Figurals)

293
OVAL BASKET

294
OVAL BASKET

295
FIBER BUNDLE

296
ZANZIBAR

297
FAN-FOOTED
SCROLL

298
SADDLE

299
WITCH'S
KETTLE

300
DAISY
KETTLE

301
FINECUT HAT

302
SWINGER

303
SWINGER

304
MANHATTAN

305
COLORADO

306
DAISY & BUTTON

307
DAISY IN
DIAMOND

308
ARCHED OVAL

309
BEAD SWAG

310
CO-OP ROYAL

293 — $28; **294** — $35; **295** — $30; **296** — $35; **297** — $25; **298** — $35; **299** — $25; **300** — $28; **301** — $30; **302** — $25; **303** — $20; **304** — $35; **305** — $45; **306** — $30; **307** — $45 (S); **308** — $40; **309** — $65; **310** — $25.

Colored Figurals

311 BEES ON A BASKET (handled)	312 BEES ON A BASKET	313 WALL BASKET	314 LAZY DAISY
315 COAL BUCKET	316 CORD & PLEAT	317 RIBBED KETTLE	318 BRITISH BOOT
319 EARLY BIRD	320 FINECUT PURSE	321 VALISE	322 BIRD BASKET
323 CHERUBS	324 ALLIGATOR	325 BOY WITH PACK	326 HORSE WITH CART

311 — $50; **312** — $50; **313** — $35; **314** — $55; **315** — $32; **316** — $38; **317** — $52; **318** — $50;
319 — $55; **320** — $40; **321** — $45; **322** — $30; **323** — $55; **324** — $50; **325** — $55; **326** — $55.

327
PEEK-A-BOO

328
TWO WOMEN.

329
LIBERTY
TORCH

330
MATCH BOOK

331
SQUIRREL & STUMP

332
DAISY & BUTTON
(fan brim)

333
DOG WITH HAT

334
GARLAND OF ROSES

335
DARWIN

336
DAISY & BUTTON
SKUTTLE

337
BABY'S BOOTEE

338
BATHING TUB

339
CANDLESTICK MATCH

340
FROG & SHELL

327 — $30; **328** — $38; **329** — $58; **330** — $40; **331** — $45; **332** — $40 (S); **333** — $40;
334 — $55 (R); **335** — $45; **336** — $28; **337** — $40; **338** — $55 (R); **339** — $45; **340** — $40.

Colored Figurals

341
BIG BEN

342
DAISY & BUTTON
MATCH BOX

343
DAISY & BUTTON
POTTY

344
KNIGHTS OF LABOR

345
SHEAF OF
WHEAT

346
BEES ON A
BASKET

347
TWO ROOSTERS

348
EARLY BIRD

349
DOG HOUSE

350
UTILITY BOOT

351
WINDSOR ANVIL

352
CORSET

353
MONKEY & HAT

354
BOY WITH PACK

355
FROG & SHELL

341 – $65 (R); **342** – $30 (S); **343** – $50; **344** – $70 (R); **345** – $65 (R); **346** – $30; **347** – $48 (S); **348** – $60 (S); **349** – $55; **350** – $38; **351** – $30; **352** – $65 (S); **353** – $48; **354** – $38; **355** – $40.

356
ATLANTA

357
MONKEY
WITH HAT

358
LIZARD

359
PLEAT
AND BOW

360
LEAF AND
PLEAT

361
PARROT &
TOP HAT

362
FROG AND
SHELL

363
HEISEY
SWEET SCROLL

364
SQUARE
FOOTED

365
HORSESHOE
AND CLOVER

366
FAN-FOOTED
SCROLL

367
BABY
OWL

368
METAL-BRIM
HAT

369
LEAF
BUNDLE

370
BEGGAR'S
HAND

371
HANGING
FLOWERS

372
NEGRO BOY

373
BASKET
MATCH

356 — $35; 357 — $45; 358 — $45; 359 — $30; 360 — $25; 361 — $35; 362 — $40; 363 — $75
(R); 364 — $22; 365 — $24; 366 — $18; 367 — $45; 368 — $23; 369 — $35; 370 — $30;
371 — $24; 372 — $45; 373 — $18.

Opaque Milk Glass

| 374 BEADED BELT | 375 FERN HEART | 376 ROSE URN | 377 BRAIDED BELT |

| 378 PAINTED MILK BARREL | 379 SIMPLE BARREL | 380 SQUARE TWIST | 381 BUNDLED CIGARS | 382 DOUBLE DOT SCROLL |

| 383 PAINTED BALL BASE | 384 WRINKLED PLEATS | 385 RIBBED BASE | 386 TWIST BASE | 387 COILING SERPENT |

| 388 SPRING SCENE | 389 PLEAT & BOW | 390 TRAMP'S SHOE | 391 TINY SCROLL | 392 LAMAR |

374 – $22; **375** – $28; **376** – $38; **377** – $35; **378** – $24; **379** – $18; **380** – $24; **381** – $24; **382** – $24; **383** – $28; **384** – $30; **385** – $22; **386** – $24; **387** – $35 (S); **388** – $30; **389** – $25; **390** – $35 (S); **391** – $12; **392** – $14.

Opaque & Milk Glass

| 393 WINDERMERE'S FAN | 394 SCROLLED SHELL | 395 BEES-IN-A-BASKET | 396 BEES-IN-A-BASKET | 397 UNCLE SAM'S HAT |

398 FOUR RABBITS   399 EAGLE'S #45   400 CARMEN   401 CORN WITH HUSKS   402 QUADRAPOD

403 MEDALLION SPRIG   404 STORK ON MILK   405 COTTAGE ON MILK   406 THISTLE ON MILK   407 DAISY ON MILK

408 WAVECREST   409 WAVECREST   410 GREENAWAY GIRLS   411 BUTTON & BULGE

393 – $45 (R); **394** – $26; **395** – $32; **396** – $38; **397** – $45; **398** – $40 (S); **399** – $28; **400** – $35 (R); **401** – $35; **402** – $30; **403** – $32; **404** – $25; **405** – $25; **406** – $25; **407** – $25; **408** – $65; **409** – $65; **410** – $45; **411** – $35.

SPECIAL ADDENDA

Illustrated on the following 24 pages are photographs which were shot for proposed future books on Northwood and Opalescent glassware. Since publication of these books has been indefinitely postponed, I am including them in this new pocket guide for your added information.

The first 12 pages consist of many popular patterns made by Northwood at four different factories from 1889 to 1910, including his location at Indiana, Pa. Northwood left this company in 1901, but the factory continued to produce glassware under the guidance of Northwood's uncle, Thomas Dugan. The factory was called the Dugan Glass Company until 1912, when the name was changed to the Diamond Glass-Ware Company. Shards unearthed at this Pennsylvania factory site can be attributed to all three of these firms, so I am grouping their patterns together in some illustrations. A history of this factory is well-documented in my Books 3 and 4.

The next 12 pages include opalescent glass items not pictured in my Book 2 and two groupings of syrups and sugar shakers not pictured in Book 3. These were photographed for proposed sequels to those volumes.

A	**B**	**C**
SWASTIKA	**DAISY IN CRISS-CROSS**	**DAISY & FERN**
$295 (R)	**$275 (R)**	**$200 (R)**

NORTHWOOD GLASS

ROYAL IVY
(FROSTED RUBINA)

1
tumbler

2
water pitcher

1
tumbler

3
pickle caster

4
butter

5
spooner

6
sugar

7
creamer

8
syrup

9
cruet

10
sugar shaker

11
individual
berry

12
master
berry

1 – $55; **2** – $295; **3** – $300; **4** – $225; **5** – $75; **6** – $165; **7** – $100; **8** – $250; **9** – $225;
10 – $120; **11** – $35; **12** – $135.

NORTHWOOD GLASS

ROYAL IVY
(CASED RAINBOW SPATTER)

13
pickle caster

14
cruet

15
sugar shaker

16
water pitcher

17
butter

18
sugar

19
creamer

20
spooner

21
individual
berry

22
master
berry

21
individual
berry

23
toothpick
holder

13 – $300; **14** – $350 (S); **15** – $175; **16** – $325; **17** – $350 (R); **18** – $175; **19** – $120; **20** – $100; **21** – $45; **22** – $175; **23** – $150.

NORTHWOOD GLASS

PANELLED SPRIG & RIBBED PILLAR

ickle caster

25
sugar shaker

26
syrup

27
cruet

28
water pitcher

29
salt

30
cruet

29
salt

31
sugar

32
creamer

33
spooner

34
butter

ugar
haker

36
toothpick
holder

37
butter

38
sugar

39
creamer

40
spooner

24 — $250; **25** — $70; **26** — $110; **27** — $120; **28** — $145; **29** — $75 pr.; **30** — $125; **31** — $55; **32** — $45; **33** — $45; **34** — $95; **35** — $120; **36** — $95 (S); **37** — $150 (S); **38** — $100; **39** — $75; **40** — $65.

NORTHWOOD GLASS

INVERTED FAN & FEATHER (PINK SLAG)

41
tumbler

42
water pitcher

43
punch cup

44
jelly compot

45
spooner

46
butter

47
sugar

48
creamer

49
individual berry

50
master berry

49
individual berry

51
salt shaker

41 – $200; **42** – $750 (VR); **43** – $120; **44** – $450; **45** – $250; **46** – $500 (R); **47** – $400; **48** – $250; **49** – $125; **50** – $450; **51** – $200.

NORTHWOOD GLASS

TEARDROP FLOWER

52
tumbler

53
water pitcher

52
tumbler

TEARDROP FLOWER

54
sugar

55
creamer

56
butter

57
spooner

GOLD ROSE

58
sugar

59
creamer

60
butter

61
spooner

52 – $38; **53** – $195 (S); **54** – $75; **55** – $50; **56** – $150 (S); **57** – $65; **58** – $85 (S); **59** – $55; **60** – $165 (R); **61** – $75.

NORTHWOOD GLASS

POSIES & PODS

62	63	64	65	64
individual berry	**master berry**	**tumbler**	**pitcher**	**tumbler**

66	67	68
spooner	**butter**	**creamer**

NORTHWOOD REGAL

69	70	71	72	73
cruet	**spooner**	**butter**	**sugar**	**creamer**

62 – $25; **63** – $125 (S); **64** – $45; **65** – $250 (R); **66** – $75; **67** – $165 (R); **68** – $55; **69** – $250 (VR); **70** – $60; **71** – $145; **72** – $85; **73** – $55.

NORTHWOOD GLASS

FLUTE
GOLDEN PEACH
MEMPHIS

74
water pitcher

75
tumbler

76
water
pitcher

77
tumbler

78
water
pitcher

MEMPHIS

79
sugar

80
spooner

81
butter

82
creamer

GOLDEN PEACH

83
butter

84
spooner

85
creamer

86
sugar

74 — $125 (S); **75** — $38; **76** — $195; **77** — $35; **78** — $165; **79** — $85; **80** — $65; **81** — $145; **82** — $50; **83** — $185; **84** — $75; **85** — $65; **86** — $120.

GLASS BY
NORTHWOOD & McKEE

PANELLED HOLLY

87	88	89	90
sugar	**butter**	**spooner**	**creamer**

GENEVA

91	92	93	94
sugar	**butter**	**spooner**	**creamer**

GRAPE AND GOTHIC ARCHES

95	96	97	98
sugar	**butter**	**spooner**	**creamer**

87 – $95; **88** – $150 (S); **89** – $50; **90** – $45; **91** – $60; **92** – $120; **93** – $45; **94** – $40;
95 – $80; **96** – $125; **97** – $50; **98** – $50.

GLASS BY
NORTHWOOD & DIAMOND

JEWELLED HEART

N. NEARCUT

PANELLED SPRIG

FAN

99	100	99	101	102	103
tumbler	pitcher	tumbler	sugar	spooner	syrup

ATLAS

104	105	106	107
sugar	butter	creamer	pitcher

INVERTED FAN & FEATHER

PANELLED HOLLY

108	109	110	111
ind. berry	master berry	ind. berry	master berry

99 – $40; **100** – $165; **101** – $75; **102** – $45; **103** – $245 (R); **104** – $55; **105** – $120; **106** – $40; **107** – $145; **108** – $35; **109** – $100; **110** – $35; **111** – $125 (S).

GLASS BY NORTHWOOD & DIAMOND

CORNFLOWER

WAVING QUILL

GRAPE WITH GOTHIC ARCH

112
tumbler

113
pitcher

114
decanter

115
pitcher

116
tumbler

N. NEARCUT

LEAF MEDALLION

FAN

117
tumbler

118
butter

119
jelly

120
tumbler

121
butter

CRYSTAL QUEEN

ALASKA

S-REPEAT

122
master berry

123
syrup

124
cruet

125
water tray

112 – $22; **113** – $125 (S); **114** – $85 (S); **115** – $165 (S); **116** – $35; **117** – $32; **118** – $145; **119** – $75; **120** – $50; **121** – $120; **122** – $100; **123** – $45; **124** – $45; **125** – $85 (R).

GLASS BY
NORTHWOOD-DUGAN-DIAMOND

DIAMOND SPEARHEAD

DIAMONDS & CLUBS

NESTOR

DIAMOND'S MAPLE LEAF

126. tumbler

127 pitcher

128 tankard pitcher

129 spooner

130 butter

131 sugar

132 creamer

133 spooner

134 butter

135 sugar

136 creamer

126 — $55 (R); **127** — $275 (VR); **128** — $85; **129** — $55; **130** — $145; **131** — $85; **132** — $55;
133 — $55; **134** — $120; **135** — $85; **136** — $45.

GLASS BY
NORTHWOOD-DUGAN-DIAMOND

S-REPEAT

CORNFLOWER

DIAMONDS CLU...

137
wine

138
decanter

140
tumbler

139
pitcher

140
tumbler

141
pitcher

S-REPEAT

142
tumbler

143
pitcher

142
tumbler

144
spooner

145
sugar

146
creamer

GOLD ROSE

DIAMOND'S MAPLE LEA...

147
butter

148
sugar

149
creamer

137 – $42; **138** – $150; **139** – $120 (R); **140** – $28; **141** – $125 (S); **142** – $35; **143** – $150; **144** – $55; **145** – $75; **146** – $48; **147** – $125; **148** – $95 (S); **149** – $65.

BLOWN OPALESCENT GLASS

HOBBS' HOBNAIL

POINSETTIA

STARS & STRIPES

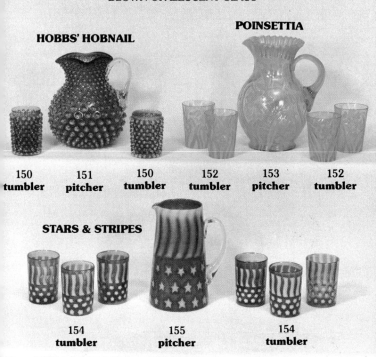

150 tumbler   **151** pitcher   **150** tumbler   **152** tumbler   **153** pitcher   **152** tumbler

154 tumbler   **155** pitcher   **154** tumbler

150 — $55; 151 — $225; 152 — $48; 153 — $175; 154 — $85; 155 — $450 (VR).

OPALESCENT GLASS PITCHERS
(Blown & Pressed)

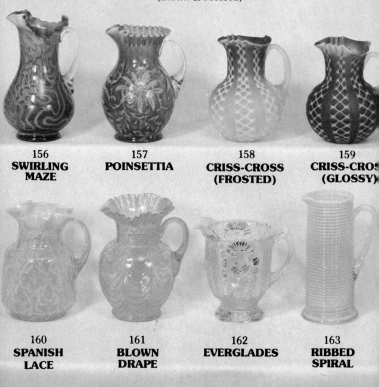

156	157	158	159
SWIRLING MAZE	**POINSETTIA**	**CRISS-CROSS (FROSTED)**	**CRISS-CROSS (GLOSSY)**

160	161	162	163
SPANISH LACE	**BLOWN DRAPE**	**EVERGLADES**	**RIBBED SPIRAL**

156 – $275 (R); **157** – $235; **158** – $375 (R); **159** – $350; **160** – $295 (R); **161** – $135;
162 – $275 (S); **163** – $250 (R).

MORE OPALESCENT GLASS
(Pressed & Blown)

64
WELLED HEART

165 **STRIPE**

166 **167**
BEATTY SWIRL

168

169
LUSTRE FLUTE

170

171
SWAG BRACKETS

172
LITTLE SWAN

173
MELON SWIRL

175
RIBBED SWIRL

174
CHRYSANTHEMUM SWIRL

176
INVERTED FAN & FEATHER

164 – $300 (R); **165** – $145 (R); **166** – $165 (S); **167** – $85; **168** – $125 (S); **169** – $200 (R); **170** – $65; **171** – $42 (S); **172** – $48 (S); **173** – $95 (VR); **174** – $38 (S); **175** – $40 (S); **176** – $250 (R).

BLOWN OPALESCENT GLASS

177
FERN

178
SPANISH LACE

179
DAISY & FERN
(REPRO)

180
BLOWN TWIST

181
SPANISH LACE

182
SPANISH LACE

183
SPANISH
LACE

184
SPANISH LACE

185
SWIRLED
HONEYCOMB

186
SEAWEED

187
BLOWN SPIRAL

177 — $250; **178** — $300 (S); **179** — $75; **180** — $285 (R); **181** — $250 (R); **182** — $225 (S); **183** — $85 (S); **184** — $125 (R); **185** — $95 (VR); **186** — $225 (R); **187** — $85 (VR).

BLOWN OPALESCENT GLASS

| 188 | 189 | | 190 **STRIPE** | 191 | 192 | 193 **CHRYSANTHEMUM SWIRL** |

N. BLOWN DRAPERY

194
SPANISH LACE

195
HOBBS' HOBNAIL

196
HONEYCOMB

197
POLKA DOT

198
SWIRL (DECORATED)

199
WINDOWS (PLAIN)

188 — $350 (R); **189** — $55 (S); **190** — $225 (S); **191** — $120 (R); **192** — $250 (S); **193** — $55; **194** — $145 (R); **195** — $145 (R); **196** — $110 (S); **197** — $245 (R); **198** — $175 (S); **199** — $265 (S).

BLOWN OPALESCENT GLASS
(Pressed & Blown)

200   201
DAFFODILS

202
WINDOWS

203   204
REVERSE SWIRL

205   206   207   208   209
NORTHWOOD REGAL

210
CIRCLED SCROLL

211
CHRISTMAS PEARLS

212   213
BUBBLE LATTICE

214
STRIPE

215
COINSPO

200 – $175 (R); **201** – $38 (S); **202** – $185; **203** – $185; **204** – $145; **205** – $195 (S);
206 – $95; **207** – $65; **208** – $75; **209** – $150 (VR); **210** – $245 (R); **211** – $175 (S);
212 – $135 (S); **213** – $145 (S); **214** – $110; **215** – $95 (S).

MORE OPALESCENT GLASS
(Pressed & Blown)

216
ANISH LACE

217
SWASTIKA
(DIAMONDS & CLUBS)

218

219
COINSPOT

220

221

222 **223**
STARS & STRIPES
(barber bottles)

224 **225**
BUBBLE LATTICE

226 **227** **228** **229** **230**
BUBBLE LATTICE **TWIST TOY SET**
(QUILTED PHLOX)

216 — $250 (S); 217 — $450 (VR); 218 — $25; 219 — $95; 220 — $25; 221 — $150 (R); 222 — $85 223 — $125 (S); 224 — $250 (S); 225 — $100; 226 — $55 (S); 227 — $95 (S); 228 — $55; 229 — $85; 230 — $135 (R).

PRESSED OPALESCENT NOVELTIES

231
OPAL HONEYCOMB

232
SQUIRREL & ACORN

233
RIB & BIG THUMBPRINT

234
JEFFERSON SHIELD

235
OLD MAN WINTER (FOOTED)

236
WILTED FLOWERS

237
LITTLE SWAN

238
DAISY MAY

239
MAY BASKET

240
SURF SPRAY

231 – $38 (S); 232 – $75 (R); 233 – $24 (S); 234 – $50 (R); 235 – $75; 236 – $35 (R); 237 – $45 (S); 238 – $28; 239 – $50; 240 – $28.

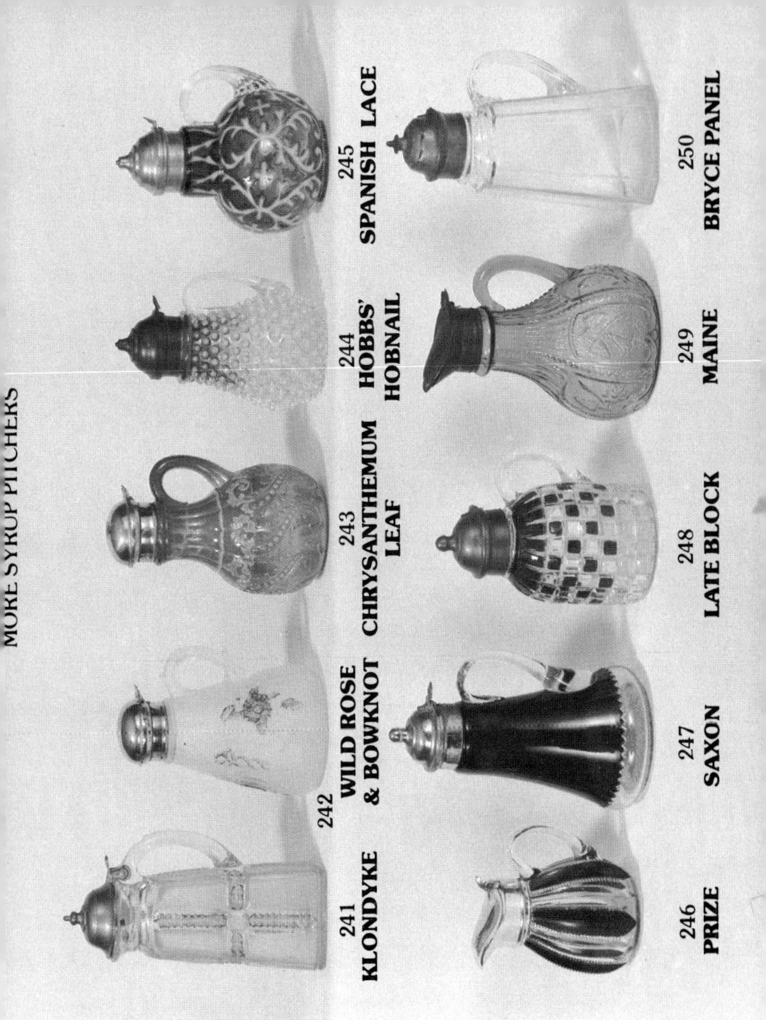
MORE SYRUP PITCHERS
241 KLONDYKE
242 WILD ROSE & BOWKNOT
243 CHRYSANTHEMUM LEAF
244 HOBBS' HOBNAIL
245 SPANISH LACE
246 PRIZE
247 SAXON
248 LATE BLOCK
249 MAINE
250 BRYCE PANEL

241 – \$650 (R); **242** – \$100; **243** – \$450 (S); **244** – \$400 (VR); **245** – \$275 (S); **246** – \$150 (S); **247** – \$120; **248** – \$145; **249** – \$250 (R); **250** – \$100.

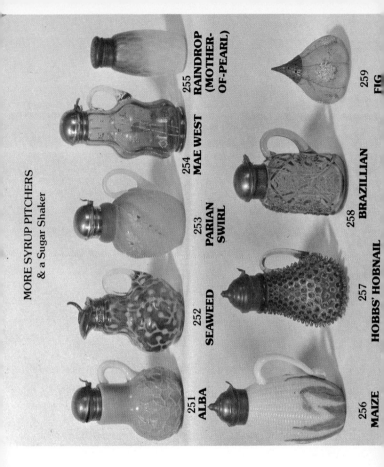

MORE SYRUP PITCHERS
& a Sugar Shaker

255
RAINDROP
(MOTHER-
OF-PEARL)

259
FIG

254
MAE WEST

258
BRAZILLIAN

253
PARIAN
SWIRL

252
SEAWEED

257
HOBBS' HOBNAIL

251
ALBA

256
MAIZE

251 – $175 (S); **252** – $250 (R); **253** – $150 (S); **254** – $165 (S); **255** – $275; **256** – $32⁵ (S); **257** – $475 (VR); **258** – $175 (S); **259** – $450 (R).

INDEX

Listed here is an alphabetical index of all patterns, novelties and color categories, followed by the pages numbers on which the items will appear.

ABBREVIATIONS: **(N)** Northwood, **(Opal)** Opalescent, **(M.O.P.)** Mother-of-Pearl, **IVT** (Inverted Thumbprint) **(D & B)** Daisy & Button **(M.W.)** Mt. Washington.

NOTES

NOTES

—have you missed
any of these books on
Victorian Colored Pattern Glass
by William Heacock?

BIG 8-1/2″ x 11″ FORMAT

5 MORE GREAT VOLUMES OF FASCINATING READING!

(with additional volumes forthcoming)

ENCYCLOPEDIA OF VICTORIAN COLORED
PATTERN GLASS, Book I – Toothpick Holders
from A to Z (Edition 2)

67 pgs., 38 full color plates in vivid detail, comprehensive research data, complete information on patterns and their makers, line drawings, information on reproductions and how to avoid them, early ad & catalogue reprints, bibliography, index, no repetition of any toothpicks shown in **"1000 Toothpick Holders."** $9.95
Accompanying price guide $1.00

ENCYCLOPEDIA OF VICTORIAN COLORED PATTERN GLASS, BOOK II – Opalescent Glass from A to Z (Edition 2)

119 pgs., 44 in brilliant color, detailed research findings on hundreds of opalescent glass patterns, comprehensive historical data, line drawings, early ad reprints, illustrations of opalescent glass reproductions, bibliography, listing of corrections & additions to text of Book I, complete index, much much more $12.95

Accompanying price guide . . . . $ 1.00

ENCYCLOPEDIA OF VICTORIAN COLORED PATTERN GLASS, Book III – Syrups, Sugar Shakers & Cruets from A to Z

96 pgs., 51 in glorious color, detailed research data on same page as accompanying illustrations, bibliography, historical data, dozens of catalogue and ad reprints (some in their original color), listing of corrections and additions to texts of Books I & II, index to first three volumes $12.95

Accompanying price guide . . . . $ 1.00

ENCYCLOPEDIA OF VICTORIAN COLORED PATTERN GLASS, Book IV—Custard Glass from A to Z (over 500 items pictured in detail)

68 pgs., 48 in vivid color, in-depth research into early custard glass production, text on same page as illustrations, featured information on Northwood's production—including color close-ups of glass shards unearthed at his Indiana, Pa. factory site, catalogue and ad reprints (some in color), listing further corrections and additions to earlier volumes $12.95

Accompanying price guide . . . . $ 1.00

ENCYCLOPEDIA OF VICTORIAN COLORED PATTERN GLASS, Book 5—U.S. Glass from A to Z (with co-author Fred Bickeheuser)

192 pgs., 24 in color, almost 4,000 different items illustrated in an incredibly detailed reprint of original company catalogues (1891-1919), so comprehensive it took two authors to compile the information, a history of the development of the United States Glass Company (a merger of 15 major companies), featuring early Duncan glass, Pittsburgh glass, Findlay glass, Wheeling glass, and hundreds of novelties, goblets, salt dips, and many patterns identified for the first time ever, a major publication in this series $14.95

Accompanying price guide . . . . $ 1.00

How about our handy pocket guide?
VICTORIAN COLORED GLASS—
PATTERNS AND PRICES—

136 pgs., in full color, an abridged version of Books 1, 2 and 3 of the "Encyclopedia of Victorian Colored Pattern Glass" in a handy pocket size, easy to carry in pocket or purse for carrying to auctions and flea markets, updated prices yearly, no separate price guide, prices on same page as illustration, index $8.95

Another Great Toothpick Holder Book!
1000 TOOTHPICK HOLDERS—

112 pgs., 6″ x 9″ format, over 1,000 toothpick holders listed, mostly in beautiful closeup color, this superb publication not only illustrates and identifies colored pattern glass, but also art glass, fine china, figurals, pressed crystal, cut glass, silverplate and bisque, sponsored by National Toothpick Holder Collectors' Society $10.95
Accompanying price guide . . . . $ 1.00

ORDER THESE PRICELESS FULL-SIZE VOLUMES
FROM YOUR FAVORITE BOOK DEALER
Or send the handy order blank with check or money order to:

ANTIQUE PUBLICATIONS, INC.
P.O. Box 655   Marietta, Ohio 45750

PLEASE RUSH ME THE FOLLOWING
BOOKS WITH MY SATISFACTION GUARANTEED!

No. copies

_____ Book 1 (Toothpicks) @ 9.95 (Hardbound – $13.95)
_____ Book 2 (Opalescent Glass) @ 12.95 (Hardbound – $16.95)
_____ Book 3 (Syrups, etc.) @ 12.95 (Hardbound – $16.95)
_____ Book 4 (Custard Glass) @ 12.95 (Hardbound – $16.95)
_____ Book 5 (U.S. Glass) @ 14.95 (Hardbound – $18.95)
_____ **1000 TOOTHPICK HOLDERS** (A Collectors Guide) @ **$10.95**
_____ Updated Price Guides for each of the above ($1 each)
_____ **VICTORIAN COLORED GLASS I** (Patterns & Prices) @ **$8.95**
_____ **VICTORIAN COLORED GLASS 2** (Patterns & Prices) @ **$9.95**
_____ (Add $.75 for postage and handling).

TOTAL AMOUNT ENCLOSED . . . . _____

Name _____

Address _____

City/State/Zip _____

127